The Industrial Relations Act at work

Joan Henderson

First published
August 1971 by
The Industrial Society
Robert Hyde House
48 Bryanston Square, London W1H 8AH
Telephone: 01-262 2401

Reprinted August 1971

Reprinted September 1971

Prices		**Examples**	
1–19 copies	75p each	20 copies	£12
20–49 copies	60p each	50 copies	£25
50–99 copies	50p each	100 copies	£45
over 100 copies	45p each	200 copies	£90

UP TO 50 COPIES ADD 1p PER COPY POSTAGE: OVER 50 POST FREE

Contents

Printed by George Berridge & Co Ltd London and Thetford

Introduction

The Industrial Relations Act 1971 will affect
the course of industrial relations in every
organisation in the country. If industry and
commerce are to gain from the Act it is vital that
all those involved — managers and trade union
officials, supervisors, foremen and shop stewards
– should have the fullest understanding of the
terms of the Act and of its practical implications
for them. They must also consider what they
need to do about it. This booklet sets out to
provide this information in the most practical
manner possible.

It is also important to realise, as The
Industrial Society has continually stressed, that
constructive management-union relations
depend above all on positive action by
management. For this reason there is a brief
check list of action points for managers.

The book has been written and priced so that
companies can make copies available to all those
who manage or represent people within the
organisation.

It has been written by Joan Henderson who was
the author of the Society's highly successful
guides to the Donovan Report and to the
Industrial Relations Bill. More than 65,000
copies of these two publications have already
been sold, a reflection of their clarity and
practical value and of the respect and support
the Society has gained from management and
the trade unions.

JOHN GARNETT

The Industrial Relations Act 1971

The purpose of the Industrial Relations Act 1971 is to provide a legal framework for the conduct of industrial relations in accordance with four guiding principles:

* free collective bargaining, conducted with due regard to the interests of the community;

* orderly procedures for the settlement of disputes which have due regard to the interests of the community;

* free association of workers in independent trade unions, and of employers in employers' associations, to regulate relations between employers and workers in a representative and responsible way;

* freedom and security for the individual.

The Act establishes the right of the worker to choose whether or not to belong to a trade union, and gives him legal safeguards against unfair dismissal from his job and against unfair treatment by a union. It outlaws the pre-entry closed shop, provides for a new 'agency shop' and an 'approved closed shop', and for legally binding collective agreements. It introduces measures for developing collective bargaining and for putting pressure on reluctant parties, and it supplements these measures with statutory procedures for resolving disputes over recognition rights, the agency shop and the disclosure of information by the employer. It establishes a new concept of 'unfair industrial practices' many of which are aimed at preventing certain kinds of strike, lockout and other forms of industrial action. These are specified throughout the Act (see Appendix 1), and legal action can be taken against any organisation or individual who commits them.

A new Registrar of Trade Unions and Employers' Associations is to be appointed to vet the rules and conduct of these organisations. Only registered organisations, which have to conform to certain standards, are entitled to specific rights and privileges. The Commission on Industrial Relations (CIR) is put on a statutory basis and given greater responsibilities. A new system of industrial relations courts is set up, with the existing industrial tribunals handling matters at the lower level, and a new National Industrial Relations Court (the Industrial Court) at the higher. The former Industrial Court is renamed the Industrial Arbitration Board and its powers of compulsory binding arbitration extended. The Department of Employment is given increased powers of conciliation.

The Secretary of State for Employment is required to prepare a code of industrial relations practice to give practical guidance on the application of the principles underlying the Act. This must be approved by Parliament, but will not be a legal document. It will, however, be used as a yardstick in legal cases. At the time of writing a consultative document on the Code of Practice has been issued for general discussion and comment (see Appendix 2). It is referred to here as the draft Code of Practice.

This book explains the main provisions of the Act and suggests some of the practical implications at the place of work. The Act's provisions are outlined in the left-hand column of each page, and their practical implications in the right-hand column.

The book is not a substitute for the full details of the Act: it is intended as a framework to assist in the understanding of a complex document.†

The Government's provisional timetable for bringing the Act into force is:

1 October Chief Registrar of Trade Unions and Employers' Associations brings into effect the provisions which deal with registration.

1 November The Commission on Industrial Relations is reconstituted as a statutory body.

December National Industrial Relations Court established and the present Industrial Court renamed the Industrial Arbitration Board.

The following provisions come into force: agency shop and approved closed shop agreements; exclusion orders for dismissal procedures; legal status of collective agreements; remedial action for defective procedures; sole bargaining agents; appeals to the court against the Chief Registrar's decisions; emergency procedures.

Early 1972 Scope of industrial tribunals extended and other provisions brought into force dealing with: trade union membership and activities; Contracts of Employment Act; unfair dismissals; disclosure of information; complaints against registered organisations; other unfair industrial practices; restrictions on legal proceedings.

---

†**Note** When referring back to the Act it is necessary to be aware of precise definitions (see Section 167) and in particular to remember that 'trade union' is used in the Act to mean a registered trade union.

(1) Union membership

The Act

5(1) Every worker has the right to belong to a registered trade union of his choice and to take part in its activities 'at any appropriate time'*, and to stand as an official. He also has the right not to belong to any kind of union. This right is not limited to particular categories of worker:

167 it applies equally to manual, white-collar and managerial staff since the term 'worker' includes anyone who is under a contract of employment.

5(2) Except where an agency shop agreement or an approved closed shop agreement is in force, it is an unfair industrial practice for an employer to refuse to engage a worker, or penalise him in any other way, for exercising his rights in relation to union membership, and for anyone to put pressure on an employer to do so. An employer will be acting unfairly if he

33(3) offers an inducement to a worker not to exercise these rights; for example, by conferring some benefit on him in order to persuade him to leave his union. But an employer may encourage workers to join a registered union which he

5(3) recognises for bargaining purposes.

106 If a worker claims that his rights in relation to union membership have been infringed, he can take his case to an industrial tribunal which can make an order declaring what his rights are in the circumstances under consideration, and can award compensation.

*__Note__ In working hours 'appropriate time' means time agreed with the employer. Any time outside the individual's working hours is 'appropriate'.

Practical implications

(1) The statutory right to join a registered trade union requires a change of policy on the part of some employers. For example:

The non-union company which has used various methods to keep trade unionists out altogether.

The company which, while countenancing trade unionism among its manual workers, has discouraged it among all its white-collar staff or among its managers.

To remove all possible doubt such employers should make it quite clear to their employees that they recognise the importance of trade unions and are prepared to co-operate fully with them if this is in accordance with the employees' wishes.

(2) Some employers are worried about their managers belonging to trade unions. But, as the Donovan Report indicated and as the experience of the Civil Service and the nationalised industries has shown, this need not lead to conflicts of loyalties, provided the manager or supervisor does not belong to the same union or section of a union as his subordinates and, in particular, is not represented by a subordinate.

(3) Some people fear that the right of the individual to choose which union (if any) he joins might result in a proliferation of unions and lead to chaos. Against this it should be noted that the right to join a union is not the same as the right to have that union recognised for bargaining purposes. There is nothing in the Act to prevent the continued operation of the TUC Bridlington principles which are aimed at defining spheres of influence between unions. (And there is nothing to prevent an individual belonging to two unions, if a union other than his own is granted recognition.)

In practice the problem is most likely to arise in areas where unions are organising for the first time. Here the possibility of proliferation will be considerably reduced if the employer grants negotiating rights at an early stage to the union (or unions) which are accepted as appropriate: he can then encourage membership of that union. In the meantime he can follow the advice of the draft Code – 'Where trade unions have not secured negotiating rights management should nevertheless be prepared to consider receiving representations from a union official on behalf of his members about grievances or other matters which can be settled on an individual basis'.

(2) Bargaining units and recognition rights

<table>
<tr><td>Section of Act</td><td>

The Act

The act provides new machinery for determining bargaining structure and recognition rights when these cannot be settled by voluntary methods.</td></tr>
</table>

*Section
of Act*

The Act

The act provides new machinery for determining bargaining structure and recognition rights when these cannot be settled by voluntary methods.

46 In cases of dispute the CIR can be brought in to make recommendations on what is an appropriate bargaining unit for a particular group of employees, and whether there should be a sole bargaining agent for that unit.

44 **A bargaining unit** means those employees who are grouped together for negotiating purposes in respect of matters not dealt with 'under more extensive bargaining arrangements'. (In addition to terms and conditions of employment, the nature of the work and the training, experience and qualifications required, are relevant factors in determining bargaining units.)

48(3)

44 **A sole bargaining agent** means the organisation of workers or joint negotiating panel (not necessarily registered trade unions) which has exclusive negotiating rights for a bargaining unit, except in matters dealt with under more extensive arrangements.

45 Applications for an examination of the bargaining structure can be made to the Industrial Court by an interested employer, one or more registered trade unions, or the Secretary of State, or by employer and unions jointly. If the Secretary of State makes the application, he must first consult the employers' and workers' organisations concerned so that they are not taken unawares. Before referring the claim to the CIR for investigation, the Court must be satisfied that it is necessary in the interests of a satisfactory settlement and that the parties have tried to reach a settlement themselves.

The CIR is given considerable discretion, but in making its recommendations it must consider whether the union or joint negotiating panel has the support of the employees concerned, as well

48(5) as the resources and organisation to enable it to represent the employees effectively (it need not be a registered union). The CIR cannot put forward as a sole bargaining agent an organisation which is not independent of the employer's

48(7) control. It can attach conditions to its recommendations; in particular, it can require a union to make sufficient trained officials available for the purposes of collective bargaining. Its report must be published.

Where the CIR recommends the recognition

Practical implications

(1) The definition of a bargaining unit, with its reference to 'more extensive bargaining arrangements', provides for situations where negotiations are conducted at different levels for different purposes.

(2) Although in this part of the Act court orders are restricted to dealing with the recognition or otherwise of sole bargaining agents, the same is not true of the CIR which can propose any suitable solution, can apply for a reference to be withdrawn if a satisfactory settlement has been reached, and can apply for a reference to be extended.

(3) Some of the uses to which the new machinery can be put are illustrated by the following examples:

(a) To compel an employer to bargain with a particular union or group of unions.

For example: Where the employer has no adequate reason for refusing to recognise the union.

Where the employer mistakenly disputes the amount of support the union has.

(b) To overcome fragmented bargaining.

For example: Where a number of unions negotiate independently for related groups of employees who would be better served by a single negotiating body. The Act's provisions for a sole bargaining agent can be instrumental in sorting these out. The solution may lie in giving exclusive bargaining rights to a joint panel of the unions, or in giving them to the one union best able to represent everybody. (No union can be forced to be part of a joint negotiating panel; but some unions, which in the past have been unwilling to sit down with others, are finding that at factory level they are no longer strong enough to act effectively on their own.)

(c) To impose a settlement where unions are competing for membership.

This would not be instead of the TUC's Bridlington procedures since, before going ahead with a reference, the Industrial Court has to be satisfied that use has been made of any available facilities for conciliation. But it would apply where the TUC procedures had failed to reach a settlement, or where they could not be used because a union involved was not affiliated to the TUC.

The Act

Practical implications

of a sole bargaining agent, either of the interested parties can apply within six months for the recommendations to be enforced, except that:

(**a**) an application cannot be made by a union which is not registered;

(**b**) no enforcement is possible if the recommended bargaining agent is not registered. The recommendations will be made legally binding (by an order of the Industrial Court) if endorsed in a secret ballot by a majority of the employees voting. The ballot is supervised by the CIR.

(d) To give support to emerging unions or other organisations of workers.

For example: Staff associations and professional groups, as well as white-collar unions, can apply for recognition if they are registered, and an employer can apply on their behalf if they are not. The fact that consideration is given to the nature of the work, and the training and qualifications of any group, gives added weight to the claims of some minorities.

(e) To provide a stepping stone for an agency shop agreement.

51

There is a similar procedure for depriving a union of exclusive negotiating rights if it is not adequately representing the employees concerned. In such a case the application can be made by any person claiming to be an employee, providing he has the written support of one-fifth of the employees within the bargaining unit (or two-fifths where the union's negotiating rights spring from a recognition order – see previous paragraph). No application will be considered within two years of a recognition order being made. Investigations will again be undertaken by the CIR who will try to promote a settlement, and where necessary conduct a ballot. If a majority of the employees voting are in favour of ending recognition of the union, the Industrial Court will make an order to that effect which will last for two years.

(4) Apart from the direct effect of the new machinery, its emphasis on the clarification of bargaining structures and on the development of exclusive bargaining rights will cause many organisations to examine their bargaining arrangements. Here one of the problems lies in identifying bargaining units. The draft Code of Practice gives some guidance. It says that there should be a substantial degree of common interest among the employees covered, and that the unit should take in as wide a group as practicable for the sake of stability and consistency. It also lists the factors which should be taken into account and makes it clear that the CIR can be brought in on a voluntary basis without going through the Industrial Court.

54 & 55

In connection with these provisions the Act specifies a number of unfair industrial practices (see Appendix 1). Not only is it an unfair industrial practice to fail to comply with a recognition order of the Industrial Court: for two years after the CIR makes a report it will be an unfair industrial practice, whether or not an order was made, to call a strike or bring other pressures to bear on an employer in order to make him recognise a union not recommended by the CIR. It is also unfair to conduct or threaten a strike or lock-out over a recognition dispute while it is before the Industrial Court or the CIR, and for the following six months. Once an order for recognition rights has been made, an employer commits an unfair industrial practice if he does not take all such action as could be expected of a ready and willing participant in collective bargaining.

A bargaining unit might consist of an industry; a whole company; a factory, office or department within a company; a local authority; a particular grade of employees; a particular occupation. Complications arise where bargaining is done in different groupings for different purposes, as for example in a multi-unit company which negotiates conditions of employment centrally while leaving each establishment to negotiate on manpower and productivity issues. It is impossible to lay down any useful general rules. Where existing arrangements are working well there is no need to disturb them. Where there is overlapping and inconsistency, or where changes are taking place in the labour force, in the company structure or in the company objectives, employers and unions can get together to work out the best way of reaching a satisfactory system of collective bargaining. If they find this impossible, the Department of Employment, the CIR and the new statutory machinery are there to assist and, where necessary, to enforce. The purpose of the Government is to provide a 'civilised alternative' to the settling of industrial relations problems by power confrontations.

(3) The closed shop

The Act

All pre-entry closed shop agreements (agreements which exclude individuals from a job unless they are already members of a union or of a particular union) are expressly outlawed. And, except in the special cases where an approved closed shop agreement is allowed (see page 7), any post-entry 100 per cent union shop agreement (by which employees are required to join the union within an agreed period after starting work) is also illegal since it infringes the worker's right not to join a union.

A worker refused employment because of a pre-entry closed shop agreement can go direct to the Industrial Court to have it declared void, and may also complain of an unfair industrial practice to an industrial tribunal.

Agency shop agreements. The Act does, however, permit an 'agency shop agreement'. This is an agreement whereby all the workers in a particular section or group must belong to a particular trade union, or, if they do not wish to be union members, must pay a contribution to the union equal to the normal subscription less optional extras: anyone objecting on grounds of conscience must pay the equivalent amount to a charity. In this way some of the advantages of the closed shop can be obtained; the union (or joint panel of unions) can negotiate for all the workers in the group; and individuals are not able to secure the benefits of union activity without paying their share, so free-riders are eliminated.

Such an agreement can be made between one or more employers and one or more trade unions, or between an employers' association and one or more trade unions, but the unions must be registered. The individual who chooses not to be a union member is not given a straight option of paying contributions to the union or paying to a charity; the latter course is possible only after conscience grounds have been established, if necessary by reference to an industrial tribunal. Non-members are permitted to ask their employer to deduct their contributions from wages or salary. An individual who fails to join the union, or to pay the appropriate contribution, can legitimately be refused employment.
Where an employer (or group of employers) is unwilling to agree to an agency shop on a

Practical implications

Agency shop agreements. (1) An agency shop is the Act's substitute for a closed shop. Its main difference is that it gives legal backing to workers to opt out of membership, though not of payment, and thereby lessens the union's control in the workplace and the union's ability to make agreements stick. It could lead to serious disturbance during a strike in which the non-members refused to join. Nevertheless, it gives the union financial security, and is likely to produce stability in union membership.

(2) The option of paying to a charity instead of to the union is likely to be granted to very few, judging by past experience of the conscience clause. For example, a union member resigning from the union would normally still have to contribute to it.

(3) On balance, rather than have an agency shop, many employers will prefer to try to achieve 100 per cent union membership on a voluntary basis, because they believe it provides better representation for the majority of employees. There is an additional practical reason: a number of unions have said they will not register and they will, therefore, not be able to make an agency shop agreement. Employers who are hoping to achieve a voluntary 100 per cent union shop will need to:

(a) make a clear statement to their employees of company policy on union membership;

(b) encourage new entrants to join the union concerned;

(c) ensure that new entrants meet the shop steward;

(d) arrange for union dues to be deducted from wages.

(4) In cases where an agency shop is appropriate and possible, employers will want to take the initiative, or at least to respond to union approaches for a voluntary agreement, so that they have some influence over the form it takes. Much depends on existing bargaining arrangements, and they may first need to be clarified or developed. It is, for example, clear that a union needs to have negotiating rights in any area where it is aiming to secure an agency shop; and it cannot obtain a ballot under the Act without them.

(5) The following are examples of situations

The Act

voluntary basis, he or the registered union or joint panel of unions concerned can apply to the Industrial Court for a secret ballot on the subject, to be held under the supervision of the CIR. If a majority of those eligible to vote, or not less than two-thirds of those voting, are in favour, then an agency shop agreement must be entered into and carried out. If the voting is against, no such agreement can be made for those workers for the next two years. Similar procedures are laid down for workers who wish to challenge the continuance of an agency shop, whether it exists by voluntary agreement or as the result of a ballot held at least two years previously. But in these cases the application for a ballot can be made by any worker who has the written support of 20 per cent of the workers covered by the agreement. And if the majority of those eligible to vote, or two-thirds of those voting, do not support the agreement, it is cancelled for at least two years.

13

14

11(3)

Only a registered union which already has negotiating rights in respect of the workers concerned can secure an agency shop through the statutory procedure.

102

A trade union can take action before the Industrial Court against an employer who has failed to implement an agency shop agreement after a ballot has decided in its favour. This is in addition to the unfair industrial practices specified in connection with the agency shop.

17

Approved closed shop agreements. The one departure from the general right of an individual not to belong to a trade union comes in the special provisions for approved closed shop agreements.

*Schedule
I*

The conditions governing such agreements are extremely restrictive. Only registered unions are eligible; the union and employer must make a joint application and submit a draft agreement; the closed shop must be justifiable as being necessary for the achievement of effective worker organisation, reasonable terms and conditions, continuity of employment and stable collective bargaining, and for the keeping of agreements. Moreover, the CIR must be satisfied that these conditions cannot be met by an agency shop. Where an approved closed shop comes into existence, the employer can dismiss, or refuse to engage, an individual who is not prepared to belong to the union other than on conscience grounds.

17(5)

Practical implications

where the issue of the agency shop might arise:

(a) Where a pre-entry or post entry closed shop has previously existed. Here it may be necessary to do nothing more than adhere to ordinary bargaining arrangements, maintaining 100 per cent union membership on a voluntary basis. Otherwise, if both sides wish it, the closed shop agreement can be replaced by an agency shop agreement provided the union or unions involved are registered.

(b) Where a number of strong unions represent different groups of employees in an organisation and negotiate separately for them. Here the agency shop can take one of three possible forms:
– a single agency shop covering the whole organisation, with the unions acting together as a joint negotiating panel;
– separate agency shops for the separate groups of employees;
– a single agency shop in favour of one of the unions and covering the whole organisation, assuming that the union has been able to get the negotiating rights either by voluntary agreement or through the procedures established under the Act (see pages 4 and 5).

(c) Where a union is establishing itself. There is no reason why an employer should not make an agency shop agreement with a union which has less than 50 per cent membership, if he is satisfied that this is in the interests of all concerned. But he should bear in mind that the agreement is open to legal challenge by 20 per cent of the workers covered, and that there is no need for them to wait for two years if the agreement is a voluntary one.

(6) There is a strong case for arranging, with the unions' consent, for the collection of union dues by deduction from wages where an agency shop is in force. It can make a shop steward's job unnecessarily difficult to expect him to collect money from people who are non-members.

Approved closed shop agreements. The approved closed shop is unlikely to affect many employers. It is intended to accommodate unions such as Equity, operating in spheres where employers are often ephemeral and employment is casual and intermittent, or unions such as the National Union of Seamen where organisation of any kind is difficult.

(4) Procedure agreements

The Act

Definition. 'Procedure agreement' is given a broad definition. It means any collective agreement, or part of it, that relates to:

(**a**) consultative, negotiating or arbitration machinery for dealing with terms and conditions of employment;

(**b**) similar machinery for dealing with other questions arising between employers and workers;

(**c**) negotiating rights;

(**d**) facilities for officials of trade unions or other organisations of workers;

(**e**) dismissal and disciplinary procedures;

(**f**) individual grievance procedures.

Notification of procedure agreements. The Secretary of State has power to make regulations requiring employers, within a specified period, to notify him of procedure agreements where they exist and to supply him with a copy or with prescribed particulars. Failure to comply with the regulations can lead to a fine of up to £100, and the provision of false or misleading information to a fine of up to £400.

Legal processes for remedial action. Where procedure agreements are defective or non-existent or are widely broken, legal remedies are available, though not in respect of a whole industry nor a whole section of an industry. They are limited to an undertaking or part of an undertaking, or to a group of associated undertakings (such as a multi-unit company or a multi-company group).

In such cases an application to the Industrial Court can be made by the Secretary of State, the employer, or a registered trade union with negotiating rights in the unit concerned. As with an application for bargaining rights, the Secretary of State must first consult the parties involved if he is the initiator, and in all cases he must offer advice and assistance to them in the hope of reaching agreement and avoiding unnecessary references to the Court. If the Court considers that the defects are such as seriously to impede orderly indutrial relations or to have caused substantial losses of working time, it can ask the the CIR to recommend suitable remedies. The CIR must promote discussions between the

Practical implications

*(**1**) Whereas the Act concentrates on measures to be taken when the absence of good procedures is damaging industrial relations, the draft Code of Practice is more positive: 'where trade unions are recognised, management should take the initiative in seeking to establish, jointly with the trade unions concerned, effective procedures for negotiation, consultation, communication and the settlement of grievances and disputes.' It also gives examples of the items to be covered:*

– a statement on which unions are recognised and on the appointment, status and functions of shop stewards;

– the constitution and scope of joint negotiating bodies and of consultative committees;

– the matters to be bargained about and the level at which bargaining should take place;

– the procedures for settling disputes;

– the procedures for handling redundancy and temporary lay-offs, as well as discipline and dismissal;

– the period for which agreements are to run and the arrangements for review and re-negotiation.

The Code leaves no doubt about management's responsibility to develop comprehensive agreements voluntarily with trade unions; and the fact that the agreements may have to be 'notified' should encourage the precision which the Code also calls for, as well as help to clarify policy.

*(**2**) Only as a last resort, when voluntary methods have broken down, and attempts to solve the problems by conciliation or voluntary reference to the CIR have failed, will the legal process be set in motion.*

*(**3**) The exclusion of industry-wide agreements (the engineering industry's York Memorandum, for example) from the legal processes – is in line with the arguments of the Donovan Report. There is a big difference between agreements made by even the largest companies and those made by an employers' association for a whole industry chiefly because an employers' association does not have the authority of a company board to control its members and back its agreements.*

The effectiveness of any procedure agreement

The Act

parties to try and get their agreement to the procedures it recommends, and if the outcome is satisfactory the matter can stop there. Otherwise the CIR must prepare a report of its findings and recommendations and send it to the Industrial Court and to the parties concerned.

41

On the application of one of the parties the CIR's recommendations can be made legally enforceable (see page 10).

depends on whether it suits local conditions. It is on the factory floor that people are disciplined and made redundant and that work practices are settled and payment systems applied. This is why the emphasis should be on factory or workplace agreements, and why large companies should leave scope in their agreements for local units to negotiate independently on those issues which can be controlled only at local level.

(4) All disputes procedures should include provision for arbitration. Despite the general exclusion of industry-wide procedure agreements from this part of the legal machinery, it would be legitimate for the CIR to recommend an industry-wide procedure as the arbitration element in a company procedure agreement.

(5) Legally binding agreements

<table>
<tr><td valign="top">

166(1)

34

35

166(4)

41

36

</td><td valign="top">

The Act

Enforceability of collective agreements.
A collective agreement means any agreement or
arrangement made between trade unions or other
organisations of workers and employers, which is
either a procedure agreement or prescribes the
terms and conditions of workers. It can be
written or oral, formal or informal. It can be
made between one or more employers and one or
more trade unions or other organisations of
workers. It includes substantive as well as
procedure agreements.

Any written collective agreement made after the
commencement of the Act will be held to be a
legally enforceable contract unless it contains an
express provision to the contrary. This applies
equally to the decisions of any voluntary joint
bodies established under a collective agreement,
but not to the decisions of a joint body on which
the employee members are not representative of
a trade union or other organisation of workers.

If a legally binding agreement is made by an
association of employers or unions, each employer
or union in the association is bound by it, unless
specifically excluded.

Imposed procedure agreements. Where,
because of defects in procedures, the CIR has
investigated and made a report (see page 8), the
procedural arrangements recommended by the
CIR can be imposed and made legally binding.
Within six months of the report's appearance
any one of the unions or employers involved may
apply to the Industrial Court for an order to this
effect to be made. (The Secretary of State may
not apply even though he initiated the original
reference.)

If all the parties wish it they can get the order
revoked or varied. If only one of the parties
wants it revoked, the Court has to be satisfied
that it is no longer necessary and may ask for
further investigation and report by the CIR.

Breaches of binding agreements. A claim for
compensation may be made against any party to
a legally binding agreement if it breaks that
agreement, or if it fails to take reasonable steps
to prevent its members taking action contrary to
undertakings given in the agreement.

</td><td valign="top">

Practical implications

Enforceability of collective agreements.
*(1) Enforcement does not only apply to the normal
range of agreements, eg industry-wide, company or
plant agreements covering traditional matters. It
can apply to agreements and arrangements made by
departmental committees, sub-committees,
consultative committees, formally constituted
meetings etc, on any matter relating to the employer-
employee situation; it embraces joint decisions on
such matters as sickness schemes, redundancy
rights and pension agreements. In any of these
cases, if a union or other organisation of workers is
acting for the employees, and if the agreement
reached is in writing it will be legally binding
unless it contains a disclaimer to the contrary. A
works committee on which the employee representa-
tives are elected by general vote, regardless of
union membership, is not affected because the
representatives are not acting on behalf of an
organisation of workers.*

*(2) Where both sides are prepared to accept
enforcement, it is necessary to ensure that the
wording of the agreement is clear enough to be
capable of enforcement.*

*(3) Where agreements are not to be legally
enforceable, the important thing is to ensure that
the written disclaimer is included. A good form of
words is: 'The parties intend that this agreement
should be binding in honour, but not that it should
give rise to any legal obligations'. It is not enough
for a body such as a works committee to issue one
disclaimer to cover all subsequent decisions. A
disclaimer must be included with every decision
recorded.*

Preventing breaches of agreements. *An
employer has to decide what steps to take to ensure
that his managers and supervisors act in accordance
with the demands of a binding agreement. These
can include:*

*(a) providing them with written details of the
agreements (in a form that is easily assimilated);*

*(b) promoting understanding of their particular
responsibilities under the agreements by discussions
and training sessions;*

*(c) drawing their attention to any ways in which
agreed procedures are not being used or agreed
conditions not being kept.*

</td></tr>
</table>

(6) Disclosure of information

<table>
<tr><td>

</td><td>

The Act

</td><td>

Practical implications

</td></tr>
</table>

	Employers have a duty to make available two kinds of information:
56	**(a)** Information necessary for all the stages of collective bargaining must be disclosed to officials or other authorised representatives of a registered trade union with whom negotiations take place. Employers will not be called upon to produce actual documents, nor to spend an unreasonable amount of time or money on preparing the information. Guidance on the principles to be followed will be given in the Code of Practice.
102	If the employer unjustly withholds information the union can apply for unilateral arbitration on the particular negotiation (see page 15) but the employer cannot be forced to disclose the information.
57	**(b)** Larger employers (at present those with more than 350 employees) will be obliged to issue to their employees an annual statement in writing giving information about the undertaking. If this information is not provided in accordance with the regulations, an employee can apply to an industrial tribunal for an order to be made, and then, if necessary, to the Industrial Court.
158	In connection with both kinds of information, an employer will not be required to disclose information which seriously prejudices the interests of the company in ways other than by its effect on collective bargaining, or to disclose information prejudicial to an individual.

The Act

Employers have a duty to make available two kinds of information:

56 **(a)** Information necessary for all the stages of collective bargaining must be disclosed to officials or other authorised representatives of a registered trade union with whom negotiations take place. Employers will not be called upon to produce actual documents, nor to spend an unreasonable amount of time or money on preparing the information. Guidance on the principles to be followed will be given in the Code of Practice.

102 If the employer unjustly withholds information the union can apply for unilateral arbitration on the particular negotiation (see page 15) but the employer cannot be forced to disclose the information.

57 **(b)** Larger employers (at present those with more than 350 employees) will be obliged to issue to their employees an annual statement in writing giving information about the undertaking. If this information is not provided in accordance with the regulations, an employee can apply to an industrial tribunal for an order to be made, and then, if necessary, to the Industrial Court.

158 In connection with both kinds of information, an employer will not be required to disclose information which seriously prejudices the interests of the company in ways other than by its effect on collective bargaining, or to disclose information prejudicial to an individual.

Practical implications

*(**1**) As the draft Code of Practice states – 'Collective bargaining can be conducted responsibly only if managements and unions have adequate information on the matters being negotiated.' The question is – what is adequate? And what is it reasonable to expect an employer to give?*

*(**2**) Full guidance will not be given in the Code until the CIR report on the subject is completed. In the meantime it is proposed in the draft Code that as a first practical step management should make available to recognised trade unions, in the most convenient form, the substance of the information which is supplied to shareholders or published in annual reports.*

*(**3**) Whatever future guidance is provided by the Code of Practice, individual employers will still need to clarify their own positions. They should be asking themselves:*

*(**a**) What information do they regard as necessary to the unions for realistic bargaining within the undertaking? For example:*

Costs – distribution, sales, production and administration (including wages and salaries).

Sales turnover – by main activities.

Profits – before and after tax.

Manpower – number of employees by jobs; rates of turnover, short-time, absenteeism, sickness and accidents.

Performance indicators – unit costs, output per man, return on capital.

Prospects and plans – new enterprises, investment plans, manpower plans.

*(**b**) What information do the unions regard as necessary, and why?*

*(**c**) How much of (**b**) will they (the employers) not disclose, and why?*

*(**d**) How much of what they are prepared to disclose are they in a position to?*

That is, do they know it themselves?

(7) Unfair dismissal

<table>
<tr><td>Section of Act</td><td></td></tr>
</table>

	The Act	*Practical implications*

The Act

Section of Act
27-30

With certain exceptions which include firms with less than four employees and employment involving less than 21 hours a week, every worker with two or more years' service and under the normal retiring age for his job is given legal protection against unfair dismissal.

22

A dismissal is <u>fair</u> if an employer has acted reasonably and has dismissed an employee for any of the following reasons:

24

(a) incapability or the absence of appropriate qualifications;

(b) misconduct;

(c) redundancy;

(d) contravention of statutory requirements;

25

(e) by way of a lock-out, as long as the individual is offered re-engagement;

26

(f) taking part in a strike, (except as in (c) of next paragraph);

6(2)

17(5)

(g) refusal to belong to a union, or to pay contributions where appropriate, when an agency shop or approved closed shop agreement is in force.

A dismissal is <u>unfair</u> if:

24(4) & 29

(a) Whatever the age or length of service of the individual or the size of the firm, it is because of the individual's membership or non-membership of a trade union or because of his trade union activities.

24(5)

(b) It is in breach of an agreed or customary redundancy procedure and there are no special reasons for departing from that procedure.

26

(c) Following strike action, other strikers are not dismissed and the reason for the dismissal is membership or non-membership of a trade union, or taking part in union activities.

24(6)

(d) Insufficient reason is shown or if the dismissal is not reasonable in the particular circumstances.

106

An individual who considers he has been unfairly dismissed can complain to an industrial tribunal, but must do so within four weeks. There is then an opportunity for conciliation, at the request of either side or at the suggestion of a conciliation officer, with a view to reaching a voluntary settlement. If the case goes on to the tribunal

Practical implications

(1) Since any individual, whatever his job and whatever his level, who feels he has been unfairly dismissed has the right to make a claim, employers will need to exercise great care over dismissals. The following questions call for particular attention:

(a) Who in the organisation has the authority to dismiss? It is essential that this is absolutely clear.

(b) What steps are taken to ensure that those with the authority to dismiss know what is 'fair'? In addition to full briefing and discussion of the subject, it is advisable for someone from the personnel function, or someone with thorough knowledge of the subject, to be available to assist in individual cases.

(c) Are works/office rules clear and known to employees? If people are to be dismissed for misconduct, they must know what constitutes misconduct.

(d) Is there an adequate disciplinary procedure in operation? It is not enough for the employer to produce one of the acceptable reasons when justifying a dismissal. He has got to show that he acted reasonably in treating it as a sufficient reason. This implies a proper system of warnings, and the opportunity for the individual to state his case and be represented. The draft Code lists points to be covered in a disciplinary procedure.

(e) Are adequate records kept of all dismissals? The employer has got to be able to show good reason. If, as often happens, the dismissal is a result of deteriorating performance over a period of time, the employer must be able to prove all the facts and not just the 'last straw'. His records should cover part-time and short service employees as well as the rest, since they may claim they have been dismissed for union activity.

(2) The provisions of the Act dealing with pressure on an employer are designed to prevent the use of intimidation to get an individual dismissed, eg, pressure by a union to secure the dismissal of an individual who refused to take part in a strike or to join the union. But these provisions are concerned only with organised pressure – ie, calling or threatening a strike or other irregular industrial action – not with peaceful argument by an individual.

(3) There are clear advantages in reaching a

The Act

Practical implications

**116(4)
& 118**

the onus of proof of the reason for dismissal is
on the employer. Where unfair dismissal is
proved, the tribunal can recommend reinstatement
if it considers it practicable, or award compensation up to a maximum of two years' pay or
£4,160 whichever is the less (see page 23). An
employer is not obliged to comply with a
recommendation for reinstatement.

33

Pressure exerted on an employer to secure an
unfair dismissal will not be accepted as justification,
but the person or organisation who has exerted the
pressure can be implicated in any legal proceedings brought against the employer and made
to pay part of the compensation.

31

Exemption from the statutory machinery can be
obtained, on application to the Industrial Court,
where satisfactory dismissal procedures have
been established by collective agreement. Such
procedures must include remedies as beneficial
as those given in the Act, and must include a
right to arbitration or adjudication by an
independent referee or body. Exemption is
available only for an agreement made by an
independent organisation of workers.

*voluntary agreement with unions on dismissal
procedures which would qualify for exemption.
In order to qualify, an agreement:*

*(**a**) must be clear about which groups of employees
it covers;*

*(**b**) must not discriminate between employees
within these groups;*

*(**c**) must provide for remedies as beneficial as
those given by the Act, though they need not be
identical;*

*(**d**) must provide for independent arbitration.*

*In addition to its greater speed and informality, a
voluntary procedure which is effective is bound to
be better in terms of industrial relations than one
imposed from outside. Here is an opportunity for
management to take the initiative in a sphere that
is relatively uncomplicated since the basic
requirements are laid down in the Act. It could
be a first step in a continuing process of voluntary
agreements which would make reliance on the law
unnecessary.*

(8) Conditions of employment

The Act

The Contracts of Employment Act 1963. Written statement of terms of employment.

The following information must be given in the written statement in addition to that already required by the Contracts of Employment Act 1963:

(a) Entitlement to holidays, including public holidays, and to holiday pay, in such a form that it is possible to calculate precisely the employee's entitlement including entitlement to accrued holiday pay on the termination of employment.

(b) An explanation of the employee's rights in relation to trade union membership (see page 3), and the effect of an agency shop agreement or an approved closed shop agreement where one is in force.

(c) The way in which an employee can take up a grievance, the person with whom he should take it up, and the subsequent steps in the grievance procedure or a reference to an accessible document which explains them.

The written statements for new employees will have to include this additional information once this part of the Industrial Relations Act is brought into operation; and within four weeks, existing employees will have to be informed of the changes through a written statement in the same way as other changes in terms of employment are notified under the 1963 Act.

Length of notice under the 1963 Act:
(a) The qualifying period for one week's notice is reduced from 26 to 13 weeks.

(b) Employees with ten years' continuous service will be entitled to six weeks' notice, those with more than 15 years' continuous service to eight weeks.

Practical implications

Contracts of Employment Act 1963.
(1) Holiday entitlement and pay. For many organisations two stages are likely to be necessary:

(a) Clarification, and possibly simplification, of policy.
This has to be done in respect of all categories of employee, and will need to cover holidays and holiday pay due in the first year of employment as well as in the last, and the methods of calculating the pay. This is a good opportunity for employers to consider eradicating the differences between white-collar and other employees, and moving towards single status, as suggested in the draft Code.

(b) The drawing up of clear statements for each grade or individual so that every employee can work out for himself what he is entitled to.

(2) Grievance procedures. The implications of the grievance procedure provisions are underlined in the draft Code of Practice when it states – 'All employees should have the right to seek redress for their grievances. Management should ensure that an effective procedure exists for them to do so, whether or not trade unions are recognised.'

The following points should be noted:

(a) All categories of employee are covered, including managers, supervisors and other staff.

(b) Where trade unions are recognised and there is an agreed grievance procedure, a separate procedure will need to be available for non-unionists, and both will have to be included in the written statement or the accessible document.

(c) A grievance procedure for non-unionists should still give the employee the right to be represented, if he so wishes, by his employee representative – see the draft Code of Practice.

(d) The requirement that a grievance procedure must specify the person to go to in the first place should be viewed in conjunction with another extract from the draft Code – 'The aim of the procedure should be to settle the grievances as near as possible to the point of origin . . . the employee should first discuss the grievances with his immediate superior.' This should give companies a valuable stimulus to re-assess the role of first line supervision.

The Act

Applications for improved terms of employment. New rights to make claims to the Arbitration Board (the old Industrial Court) for improved terms and conditions of employment are given to registered trade unions. The Industrial Court can authorise a claim:

125

(**a**) if it finds that the employer has failed to negotiate seriously with the union stipulated in a recognition order (see page 5);

126

(**b**) if it finds that the employer has failed to disclose to trade union representatives the information necessary for collective bargaining (see page 11).

In these claims it is for the union to specify the terms and conditions it is seeking and the employees affected.

152(2)

Claims for recognised terms or conditions of employment, under the Terms and Conditions of Employment Act 1959, can now be made in respect of workers in Wages Council industries, who were previously excluded.

Practical implications

Claims to the Arbitration Board. *These provisions introduce sanctions against employers who neglect their responsibilities for collective bargaining in the two ways described. If employees' pay and conditions suffer as a result of that neglect, they can be adjusted by unilateral arbitration. No restriction is put on the claim a union may make. This is in contrast to a claim made under the Terms and Conditions of Employment Act 1959 which is limited to cases where terms and conditions are less favourable than those established in the industry or section of industry concerned.*

(9) Registration and the unions

<table>
<tr><td>Section of Act</td><td>

The Act

Registration is conditional on the acceptance of minimum standards as to rules and members' rights: in return it confers rights and privileges on the registered organisation.

</td><td>

Practical implications

</td></tr>
</table>

Section of Act

The Act

Registration is conditional on the acceptance of minimum standards as to rules and members' rights: in return it confers rights and privileges on the registered organisation.

67

Requirements of registration. For an organisation to be a registered trade union it must:

- be an independent organisation of workers;

- have power to alter its own rules, and to control the use of its own property and funds.

65

The following basic principles affecting members' rights must be embodied in the rules of the organisation:

(**a**) no arbitrary exclusion from membership of an individual who is appropriately qualified to do work ordinarily done by members of the particular union;

(**b**) no restriction on the right of an individual to resign from the union if he has met his obligations – eg given reasonable notice;

(**c**) the equal right of every member to hold office, nominate candidates, vote in elections or ballots, and participate in meetings;

(**d**) the equal right of members to vote without interference, and to vote secretly when a ballot is used;

(**e**) the right of every member (except in cases of non-payment of subscriptions) to have written notice of any charge against him, time to prepare his defence, a fair hearing and a written statement of the findings before he can be disciplined;

(**f**) no restriction on the right of a member to institute proceedings in any court or tribunal or to appear as a witness;

(**g**) no right for the union to discipline a member because he has refused to take part in any 'unfair industrial practice', or because he has refused to take part in a strike not connected with an industrial dispute.
(These principles have to be followed by any organisation of workers registered or not.)

Schedule 4

The rules must also cover a number of specific matters including:

(**a**) the manner of appointment and removal of

Practical implications

Although the system of registration applies to employers' associations as well as to trade unions, it is the unions who will feel its full effect. Many of the provisions are not relevant to employers' associations, and many employers are outside employers' associations. Whereas trade unions are essential for the purposes of collective bargaining, employers' associations are not. These notes therefore concentrate on the effects of registration on unions.

Requirements of registration.

(**1**) An employer-dominated or employer-financed union or staff association cannot achieve registration since it is not independent. Nevertheless, there are active staff associations which, if not already independent, are prepared to make themselves so in order to be able to apply for registration.

(**2**) The requirements of registration directly affect the position of shop stewards and other workplace representatives. Not only must their powers and duties be specified in the union rules; the circumstances, if any, in which they can call a strike or any other industrial action must be spelt out. In practice this could lead to considerable restrictions of shop steward activities:

(**a**) a union may hesitate to give its stewards authority to make agreements which could become legally enforceable, if only by mistake;

(**b**) a union is unlikely to delegate to shop stewards the power to call a strike because of the financial risk in terms of strike pay and of possible claims on union funds resulting from unfair industrial practices;

(**c**) a shop steward acting outside the scope of his authority could be liable as an individual for an unfair industrial practice and be faced with a demand for compensation. He may therefore err very much on the side of caution in implementing the rules which define his authority.

While there is a need for the functions and authority of shop stewards and workplace representatives to be clarified, it would be a serious matter if shop stewards were shackled. Employers rely heavily on them to get speedy response to fast-changing circumstances, as well as to achieve steady change as in a long-term productivity agreement. Inquiries have shown that where managers have a choice of dealing with either full-time officers or shop stewards, three-

The Act

principal officers, and of shop stewards or other workplace representatives;

(**b**) their powers and duties;

(**c**) the body or official which may instruct members to strike or take other industrial action, and the circumstances in which such instruction may be given;

(**d**) the reasons for taking disciplinary action, the nature of the action, and the procedure to be followed, including provision for appeals.

81 & 107 Complaints to the Registrar about any breach of the basic principles or of the rules of the union can be made by any person who is a member of the union, or who was a member and has been forced to leave, or by anyone who has been refused admission to membership. The Registrar can if necessary pass on a complaint to an industrial tribunal or to the Industrial Court.

108
103 Compensation can be awarded and, in the last resort, a union can be deregistered.

Practical implications

quarters of them choose shop stewards. Besides, there are just not enough full-time officials to do the job which shop stewards do.

***What if unions choose not to register?** In March 1971 at a special Trade Union Congress a resolution was passed to the effect that all trade unions affiliated to the TUC should be advised not to register and if they decided to register to discuss the matter first with the General Council. Some unions will need to register in self-protection: for example those, like NUBE and NALGO, facing strong competition from a staff association or a professional association which itself may register; or those, like Equity, who need to apply for an approved closed shop agreement. But at the time of writing several of the major unions have declared they will not register.*

How will this affect the employers who deal with these non-registered unions?

*(**a**) If existing negotiating arrangements are satisfactory they can continue undisturbed, unless an agency shop (or approved closed shop) agreement is sought. This cannot be concluded, even on a voluntary basis, with an unregistered union.*

*(**b**) Where there are conflicts over recognition rights, an unregistered union or panel of unions can be made the sole bargaining agent by voluntary agreement. If necessary, an employer can apply to the Industrial Court for an unregistered union to be made the sole bargaining agent, and as long as it is an independent organisation the CIR can recommend it; but there can be no legal enforcement.*

*(**c**) The legal enforceability of collective agreements applies equally to agreements made with unregistered as with registered unions.*

*(**d**) Although the powers and duties of shop stewards and other workplace representatives do not have to be specified in the rules of an unregistered union, these representatives are much more vulnerable at law than those in a registered union. At the same time the basic principles affecting members' rights have to be adhered to by an unregistered union.*

Section of Act	The Act	*Practical implications*

<table>
<tr><td valign="top">*Section of Act*</td><td></td><td></td></tr>
</table>

The Act

Practical implications

Benefits of registration. (a) The protection under the law in respect of acts done in furtherance of industrial disputes is restricted to registered organisations and their officials. It is an unfair industrial practice for any other organisation or individual to induce people to break their contracts, eg, to strike without due notice in furtherance of an industrial dispute.

(b) Only registered unions can make a claim for exclusive bargaining rights under the Act, or be granted enforceable bargaining rights. (The employer or the Secretary of State may, however, claim on behalf of a non-registered union.)

(c) Only a registered union can operate an agency shop (voluntary or statutory) or an approved closed shop.

(d) Only the representatives of registered unions are entitled to the information which the Act requires employers to disclose for the purpose of collective bargaining.

(e) Only registered unions can initiate a claim for improved terms and conditions under the Act or under Section 8 of the Terms and Conditions of Employment Act 1959.

(f) There are upper limits on the compensation that can be awarded against a registered union, but not against an unregistered one.

(g) The right of the individual to belong to a union of his choice and to take part in its activities applies, in relation to his employer, only to registered unions.

Procedure for registration. Any trade union registered under existing legislation will be transferred automatically to a provisional register. Unless it is ineligible for full registration because it is not independent or because its rules are unsatisfactory, the Registrar will transfer it at the end of six months to the register established by this Act. Thereafter the union can be struck off the register at its own request, or by order of the Industrial Court.

Benefits of registration. (1) It is frequently claimed that only registered unions will continue to get the tax exemption traditionally enjoyed in respect of provident benefits. The position is that a union which does not register is able to hive off its provident funds into a separate organisation and register it as a friendly society, thereby achieving comparable advantages but at the cost of giving up control over these funds and access to them.

(2) Since the right of the individual to take part in union activities at work is limited to registered unions, an employer could legally refuse to allow a shop steward of an unregistered union to engage in union activities in working hours.

Section of Act references: 96; 45(2), 49(2); 11; 56; 152(1); 125 & 126, 117; 5(1a); 78 & 79

The Act

The Special Register. Certain chartered bodies
and registered companies, which consist wholly
or mainly of workers and may negotiate on behalf of
their members, but which cannot register as
trade unions, can apply to go on a special register
and thereby secure the same benefits as a
registered trade union. They also become subject
to the same obligations.

Practical implications

*The Special Register. This register is intended
for professional organisations who cannot register
as trade unions either because they are companies
registered under the Companies Act, or incorporated
by charter or letters patent, or because the
regulation of relations between workers and
employers is not one of their principal objects.*

(10) The right to strike

<table>
<tr><td valign="top">

</td><td valign="top">

The Act

A distinction is made between the freedom of the individual to take part in a strike himself, and his freedom to cause other people to strike – that is, his freedom to organise a strike. The new restrictions on striking are aimed at the latter. They affect the leaders of strikes.

The right to call or organise a strike. The main restriction arises out of the 'unfair industrial practices'. The Act specifies a number of circumstances in which it is an unfair industrial practice for a trade union or other organisation of workers, or for an individual, to call a strike or organise irregular industrial action short of a strike, or to threaten to do so (see Appendix 1).

97 & 98   They include industrial action in support of an unfair industrial practice, as well as sympathetic strikes and secondary boycotts against someone who is not a party to the dispute and has not given material support to one side. In respect of these unfair industrial practices, legal proceedings

101   can be taken against any individual or organisation.

96   One major unfair industrial practice does not apply to registered unions. This makes it an unfair industrial practice for anyone other than registered trade unions, and officials acting within the scope of their authority, to induce a breach of contract in contemplation or further-ance of an industrial dispute. If any other persons or organisations – an unofficial leader or an unregistered union, for instance – call a strike in these circumstances and thereby cause workers to break their contracts of employment, they commit an unfair industrial practice and are liable for legal action.

101   The initiative for taking legal action rests with the employer or other injured person. There is a ceiling on the amount that can be awarded against a registered trade union but not otherwise. (see page 23).

138 &   **Government intervention.** In emergency
139   conditions where a strike is likely to endanger the national economy, national security, public health or public order, the Secretary of State can apply to the Industrial Court for an order to defer the strike for up to 60 days. In such conditions, or in circumstances where the livelihood of a substantial number of workers in an industry is seriously threatened, he can also

</td><td valign="top">

Practical implications

The right to call or organise a strike

(1) It is helpful to look more closely at some of the phrases used:

(a) 'Irregular industrial action short of a strike.' This is defined in the Act as being conduct by a group of workers (in contemplation of furtherance of an industrial dispute) which is intended to interfere with the production of goods or services and is in breach of their contracts of employment.

(b) 'To induce another person to break a contract.' Part of a contract of employment is the amount of notice that has to be given to terminate it. The same amount of notice has to be given if a worker is to strike without breaking his contract, and if a number of workers are involved it is the longest notice of any of them that has to be given. A worker can also break his contract by going slow, or by an overtime ban if a certain amount of overtime is obligatory. A work to rule does not usually involve a breach because employees are keeping strictly to the letter of their contracts.

(c) 'In contemplation or furtherance of an industrial dispute.' 'Industrial dispute' means a dispute between a workers' organisation and an employer or employers' organisation. It does not mean a dispute between workmen and workmen, as 'trade dispute' did in the 1906 Act, now repealed. So a strike arising from inter-union competition in which the employer is not in any way involved does not qualify for protection. Nor does a purely political strike.

(2) The following indicates in broad terms the position of those who organise strikes:

(a) Any strike (or other irregular industrial action) is illegal if it is an unfair industrial practice or is in support of an unfair industrial practice, whether or not proper notice is given, and whether or not it is called by a registered union.

(b) Apart from this a registered union or its authorised officials can call any strike (or induce a breach of contract in some other way) without notice, as long as it is connected with an 'industrial dispute'.

(c) Anyone other than a registered union or its authorised officials, eg an unregistered union, or someone in a registered union who has no authority to call a strike – has to give proper notice of a strike.

</td></tr>
</table>

The Act

apply to the Court to authorise a ballot if there is doubt about whether the workers involved support the strike. The result of a ballot will be published but there is no provision for it to be made binding.

The right of the individual to strike. The individual is free to strike subject only to the requirements of his individual contract of employment. Due notice of a strike given by, or on behalf of, an individual (for example by a union official), is not a breach of contract unless the contract expressly provides otherwise. No court can compel an individual to take part in a strike or other industrial action, nor can it compel him to return to or remain at work.

An individual can be fairly dismissed for going on strike, providing others who went on strike are also dismissed and he is not being singled out because of his trade union activities.

Picketing. The protection which the law gives to peaceful picketing will no longer apply to picketing a person's home.

Practical implications

That is, lightning strikes can be called with impunity only by authorised officers of registered unions.

(3) Some examples:

(a) An authorised official of a registered union refuses to allow his members in firm A to handle components from a separate firm, B, where there has been a long, official strike over job grading. Illegal, because he is taking action against firm A which is not connected with the original dispute and this is an unfair industrial practice.

(b) A shop steward of a registered union, with no authority to call a strike, calls one without notice because of the obviously unfair dismissal of someone on his section. Illegal, because he is not acting within the scope of his authority. (He would be in the clear legally if he gave proper notice, even though it might still be an unofficial strike, without backing from his union.)

(c) A 'militant', with no standing in any union, brings out his section after a week's notice because the workshop is draughty. No legal objection provided none of the strikers is on more than a week's notice.

(d) An authorised official of an unregistered union which has exclusive bargaining rights in a large company, gives a month's notice of a companywide strike in an attempt to ward off redundancies. Illegal if any of the strikers are obliged to give more than a month's notice.

(11) Legal processes

<table>
<tr><td>

The Act

The new system. Industrial relations matters are in general to be dealt with by the new National Industrial Relations Court (called the Industrial Court) and, beneath it, by the existing industrial tribunals which already deal with matters arising from the Contracts of Employment Act 1963, the Industrial Training Act 1964 and the Redundancy Payments Act 1965 and will later deal with the Equal Pay Act 1970. Action in these courts has to be initiated by the person who believes he has grounds for complaint. In any proceedings the Code of Practice will be taken into account, where relevant, by the Court or tribunal in reaching a settlement.

Industrial tribunals. The industrial tribunals will deal with matters affecting individuals including:

(**a**) the failure of an employer to disclose the stipulated information to an employee;

(**b**) unfair industrial practices relating to dismissal and to infringement of rights in connection with trade union membership;

(**c**) the failure of a union or employers' association to meet the requirements on the way the organisation is run. (Alternatively these cases can go to the Registrar.)

The tribunals will have power:

– to make an order determining the rights of the individual and of the employer or organisation concerned;

– to award compensation in connection with (**b**) and (**c**) above.

The Industrial Court. The Industrial Court will deal with:

(**a**) All complaints about unfair industrial practices other than those covered by (**b**) and (**c**) above.

(**b**) Cases transferred from the industrial tribunals and from the Registrar.

(**c**) Appeals from the industrial tribunals on points of law and from decisions of the Registrar.

(**d**) Cases concerned with the effect of, or the enforcement of, a collective agreement.

(**e**) Applications for statutory sole bargaining rights, agency shop agreements, approved closed shop agreements, imposed procedures.

</td><td>

Practical implications

*(**1**) The fact that the Code of Practice is to be taken into account in legal proceedings is very relevant to employers and unions, and could affect the amount of compensation awarded for or against them. Favourable treatment by the Court or by a tribunal is unlikely, for example:*

*(**a**) For an employer who without warning makes drastic changes in working conditions and thereby provokes a strike. (The draft Code states that it is important for employees' views to be sought on proposed changes which would affect them.)*

*(**b**) For a union whose officials have been so obstructionist as to make proper negotiation impossible. ('Trade unions should . . . co-operate with individual managements in establishing effective procedures for negotiation, consultation, communication. . .')*

*(**2**) In practice, unions and employers are hardly likely to indulge in a spate of legal actions. Where they do take proceedings it will most probably be in connection with strikes, and the main interest then will be to get people back to work on reasonable terms, if necessary by a court order. Threats of large awards of compensation will only worsen shop floor relations. And the likelihood of an employer recovering a large sum is not very great, except in the case of an official strike backed by a registered union. Where the individual strike leader (as opposed to the union) has to pay, he may not have the money, and in many situations it will be impossible to identify him anyway.*

*(**3**) Compensation is much more relevant where individual rights are involved because in these cases, particularly dismissals, the monetary loss can be very serious to the individual.*

</td></tr>
</table>

The Act

The Industrial Court will have power:

– to make an order determining the rights of the parties;

– to award compensation;

– to make a restraining order to stop someone acting in a particular way. (This is a power the tribunals have not got.)

But the Industrial Court and the industrial tribunals must ensure that the people before them have had the opportunity to avail themselves of the services of conciliation officers.

Amounts of compensation. The compensation awarded by the courts to an injured party is payable by the person or organisation responsible for the injury. In cases concerning the infringement of individual rights, either by an employer in relation to an employee, or by an organisation of workers or employers in relation to a member (see (**b**) and (**c**) of the paragraph 'Industrial

tribunals' above), the maximum compensation that can be awarded to an individual is 104 weeks' pay or £4,160 (ie, 104 weeks at £40),

which ever is the less. A limit is also set on the compensation which can be awarded against a registered trade union as follows:

£5,000 for a union with less than 5,000 members;
£25,000 – between 5,000 and 25,000 members;
£50,000 – between 25,000 and 100,000 members;
£100,000 – over 100,000 members.

Otherwise there are no limits on the amounts that can be awarded against any organisation, company or individual.

Compensation is assessed on the basis of the loss sustained by the injured party as a result of the action complained of, but can be increased in cases of unfair dismissal where the employee has been refused reinstatement.

Enforcement. An award of compensation which the offender fails to pay is enforceable in the same way as any other civil debt, through the county courts. It cannot lead to imprisonment, but can lead to attachment of earnings.

Refusal to comply with a restraining order can be dealt with in various ways by the Industrial Court, but it can, in the last resort, lead to imprisonment for contempt of Court.

Legal aid. Legal aid will be available in the ordinary way to persons appearing before the Industrial Court, but not before industrial tribunals.

Unfair industrial practices Appendix (1)

Both management and unions are concerned to know how far people are free to call strikes or cause workers to take other forms of industrial action. The list of unfair industrial practices set out below is arranged so as to make this clear. The left hand column contains those actions by trade unions or other organisations of workers or by individuals which constitute unfair industrial practices; the right hand column lists the corresponding unfair practices on the part of management. The numbers indicate the section of the Act.

It will be an unfair industrial practice for a trade union or other organisation of workers or for an individual to call a strike or organise irregular industrial action short of a strike, or to threaten to do so, in the following circumstances:

Corresponding unfair industrial practice on the part of an employer or employers' association.

(**1**) In order to induce an employer to discriminate against any worker or applicant for work on the grounds of his membership or non-membership of a union. 33(3)

To infringe a worker's right to join (or not join) a union and take part in its activities; to refuse to employ a person because of his union membership or non-membership (except where there is an agency shop or approved closed shop agreement). 5(2)

(**2**) In order to secure the unfair dismissal of any employee. 33(3)

To dismiss an employee unfairly. 22(1)

(**3**) In support of any other unfair industrial practice. 97

To conduct or threaten a lock-out for the same purpose. 97

Agency shop and closed shop agreements
(**4**) In order to prevent an application for a ballot on an agency shop. 16(2)

To conduct or threaten a lock-out for the same purpose. 16(1).

(**5**) In order to induce an employer to make an agency shop agreement once an application for a ballot has been made. 16(2)

———————

(**6**) In order to prevent an employer making an agency shop agreement after a ballot has decided in favour. 13(2)

———————

(**7**) In order to induce an employer to enter into or continue a pre-entry closed shop agreement. 33(3)

———————

(**8**) In order to induce an employer to join in making an application for an approved closed shop agreement. 33(3)

———————

Recognition rights
(**9**) In furtherance of a recognition dispute which is before the Industrial Court or the CIR and for six months after the CIR has reported; or once the Secretary of State has accepted that an application should go to the Industrial Court. 54(4)

To conduct or threaten a lock-out for the same purpose. 54(4)

(**10**) In order to prevent an employer negotiating seriously with the sole bargaining agent specified in a court order, or to make him negotiate with some other organisation. 55(3)

To fail to negotiate seriously with the sole bargaining agent specified in a court order, or to negotiate with some other organisation. 55(1)

(**11**) In order to prevent an employer withdrawing recognition from a union in contravention of a court order. 55(7)

To conduct or threaten a lock-out to prevent an application to the Industrial Court for recognition of a sole bargaining agent or withdrawal of such recognition. 55(8)

(**12**) In order to induce an employer, within two years of a CIR report on recognition, to recognise a union other than that recommended in the report. 55(6)

In addition to the above list (in which strikes and irregular industrial action are specifically mentioned) it will also be an unfair industrial practice:

(**13**) For anyone other than a registered trade union or a registered employers' association to induce others to break a contract in furtherance of an industrial dispute. 96(1)

(**14**) For anyone to try and secure a breach of contract other than a contract of employment, or to interfere with the performance of such a contract, against someone who is not connected with the original dispute. 98

(**15**) For a party to a legally enforceable collective agreement to break it, or to fail to take all reasonable steps to prevent its members taking action contrary to undertakings given in the agreement. 36(102)

(**16**) For any workers' organisation or employers' association (registered or not) to act in contravention of the Act's guiding principles governing the conduct of such organisations. 66

Introduction
One of the provisions of the Industrial Relations Act is the issue of a Code of Practice, the purpose of which – to quote the Secretary of State for Employment – is 'to set standards and give practical guidance in the conduct of industrial relations and the development of policies to improve human relations in all types of employment'. Nothing in the Code is enforceable by law, but it will be admissible in evidence in proceedings that go before the National Industrial Relations Court or industrial tribunals.

When the Industrial Relations Act received the Royal Assent in August 1971, the Code had been issued as a consultative document. The final approved form of the Code is not likely to be issued much before the end of 1971. This appendix is therefore a summary of the contents of the consultative document. When the Code is published in its final form, this appendix will be altered accordingly for subsequent reprints of this book.
The draft Code covers much wider ground than that covered by the Act, which is a reminder that constructive management-union relations must be considered in the context of all that goes on at the place of work. The draft Code is divided into seven sections, each of which is briefly summarised below, together with some of the key points in each.

(A) Responsibilities. The responsibilities of management, trade unions, employers' associations, and of the individual employee, are defined separately. 'Primary responsibility' for good industrial relations is placed upon management and this is seen as covering the development of 'fair and effective personnel and industrial relations policies', effective organisation of work and the provision of training in industrial relations for all members of management who have a major responsibility for collective bargaining. The supervisor is identified as a key member of management. Union organisation and internal communication are examined as well as union aims.

(B) Employment policies. There are individual sections on: planning and use of manpower; recruitment and selection; training; payment systems; status and security of employees; working conditions.

The draft Code lays particular stress on the need for soundly based pay policies and systems, since the lack of these is a frequent cause of disputes. Differences between employees that are not related to the responsibilities of the job should, the draft Code say, be progressively removed. Thus the draft Code points the way to single status.

(C) Communication and consultation. The need for systematic communication down the line to employees is emphasised and the essential information that each employee needs is listed. Face to face communication is identified as the most important method of communication. There are guide-lines on the establishment and operation of consultative committees and the draft Code stresses the need to link negotiation with consultation.

(D) Collective bargaining. The draft Code recognises the importance of industry level negotiations but concentrates on collective bargaining at the place of work. It lays down guide-lines on the nature, composition and establishment of 'bargaining units'. It lists the factors affecting recognition of trade unions and indicates what management's responsibilities are after recognition. It differentiates between industry level negotiating procedures and those at the place of work. It distinguishes between procedure agreements and substantive agreements and indicates what each type of agreement should contain. Facilities for trade union activities and the status and function of shop stewards are among those matters which the draft Code says should be included in a procedure agreement. It describes the stages that might be included in a procedure for settling disputes through to conciliation and arbitration.
On disclosure of information the draft Code states that management should try to meet all reasonable requests from trade unions for information relevant to a negotiation. (Further guidance will be given on this after the Commission on Industrial Relations has completed its current enquiry on the subject.)

(E) Shop stewards. The draft Code states that the arrangements for the appointment of shop stewards and their status and function are important for good industrial relations and there

are sections on: appointment and qualifications;
status; functions; facilities; senior shop stewards
and convenors; training. The issue of joint
credentials, the steward's responsibility for
observing agreements, the minimum facilities
to enable him to do his job as a representative
are some of the matters covered. Both management and the trade unions are identified as
having responsibilities for the training of
stewards and guide-lines are given on what
these responsibilities are.

(F) Individual grievance procedure. The aim
of the individual grievance procedure is stated
as 'to settle the grievance as near is possible to
the point of origin' and the characteristics of a
grievance procedure are listed.

(G) Disciplinary procedures. 'Management
should ensure that a fair and effective procedure
exists for dealing with disciplinary matters.' The
rules of work should be made known as well as
the disciplinary action that might follow if the
rules were broken. The draft Code lists the
characteristics of a disciplinary procedure,
eg the steps involved, the right to union
representation, the need for written records, the
right of appeal.

Note
Copies of the draft Code are available free at
employment exchanges throughout Great
Britain and from the regional and headquarter
offices of the Department of Employment.
The Secretary of State has asked for comments
on the draft Code from interested organisations
and individuals. The closing date for these is
18 October 1971.

Responsible employers are not seeking to use the Industrial Relations Act to take legal proceedings against their employees or employee representatives. Nor are they expecting the Act to produce the kind of changes in industrial relations that can only result from good management.

They have two principal aims. To ensure that their existing policies and practices conform to the provisions of the Act. And to see how they can use the Act and the Code to make industrial relations more productive.

What action should managements be taking? The following check list sets out a number of proposals:

(**1**) Discuss the implications of the Act and the Code on company policy and practice with all levels of management and with representative bodies, and get them to identify particular problems.

(**2**) Clarify company policy towards trade unions, including white-collar unions, bearing in mind that one of the objectives of the Act is to encourage the development of freely conducted collective bargaining. Issue a statement on this.

(**3**) Decide whether to aim for maximum union membership on a voluntary basis.

(**4**) Clarify bargaining units. That is, which employees are best grouped together for bargaining purposes?

(**5**) Ensure that the individual grievance procedure (for union members and non-members) is satisfactory, and that it is in a written form which can be made available to employees.

(**6**) Examine recruitment policy and practice to ensure that it does not infringe the Act's provisions.

(**7**) Examine dismissals policy and procedure. Does the policy meet the requirements of the Act, and is the procedure adequate regarding warnings and records?

(**8**) Consider the introduction of a voluntary dismissals procedure which is good enough to provide exemption from the statutory machinery on dismissals.

(**9**) Assess the effectiveness of plant-level procedural agreements, and if necessary renegotiate them.

(**10**) Consider the type of information about the organisation which employees should be given regularly, and which shop stewards or trade union officials should be given to make negotiations more constructive.

(**11**) Clarify contracts of employment, particularly on matters like works rules and conditions governing overtime, so that it is possible to tell when a breach of contract has occurred.

(**12**) Consider whether to aim for legally binding agreements.

(**13**) Examine the facilities given to shop stewards to see whether they need improving.

(**14**) Determine industrial relations training needs – for supervisors and managers and for employee representatives.

(**15**) Conduct intensive communication programme on the Act throughout the organisation.